VIETNAM

A PORTRAIT

Published by: Elsworth Books
407 Yu Yuet Lai Building,
43–55 Wyndham Street,
Hong Kong.
© 1994, Elsworth Books Ltd
First edition
ISBN 962-7787-02-7

Publisher: Paul Andrews
Project Director: Tim Hall
Special Consultant: Richard Lund
Honorary Chairman: Dr Boon Vanasin
Editor: Robyn Flemming (Wordswork Ltd)
Photo Editors: Caroline Robertson & Hilda Gill
Designer: Desmond Quilty (EQ Design)
Printed in Hong Kong by Twin Age Ltd

Special thanks to all who made this book possible including:
Barry Shea: (Pepsi), Dominique Nordmann (Omni Saigon Hotel), Alex F. Kiljan Van Heuven (Tiger Beer),
Luzi Matzig (Diethelm Travel), Alex Mckinnon (Vietnam Investment Review).
Also thanks to: Press Department, Ministry of Foreign Affairs, Elly Darley, David and Anh, Phat, Mr Binh, Doung,
Ray Faasen-Intabex, Frédéric Le Page, Philippe and Daryneth Lenain, Koh Tai Hong, Oliver Wheatcroft,
Duncan Lardner, Alexander Egert, Alessandra Egert, Ciara Shannon, Tracey Hewison, Natasha Durlacher,
Alex Creswell-Turner, Elisa Laguatan, Hoang Nguyen Thuy Hoang, Dao Huu Loan, James Spurway,
Piet and Carine Steel, Ms Yanna.

Cover: A young girl peers out from under the brim of her hat at a market near Ho Chi Minh City.

An elderly woman in Hoi An (right).

*Following pages: Women transplant rice seedlings in paddy fields near Hue; Dusk casts a final
luminescent glow over the plains near Hue; One of many statues of revolutionary leader
Ho Chi Minh, with the People's Committee Building in the background, in the city named for him;
A woman awaits the morning fishing trawlers of Phu Quoc Island.*

VIETNAM
A PORTRAIT

Main photographs by
Tim Hall
and
Alain Evrard

Text by
Jacques Bekaert

Captions by
Frances Bartlett

Elsworth Books

OMNI 🏵 SAIGON HOTEL
VIETNAM

DIETHELM
TRAVEL

Tiger BEER

**Vietnam
Investment Review**

INDÔCHINE
1 9 2 9

Contents

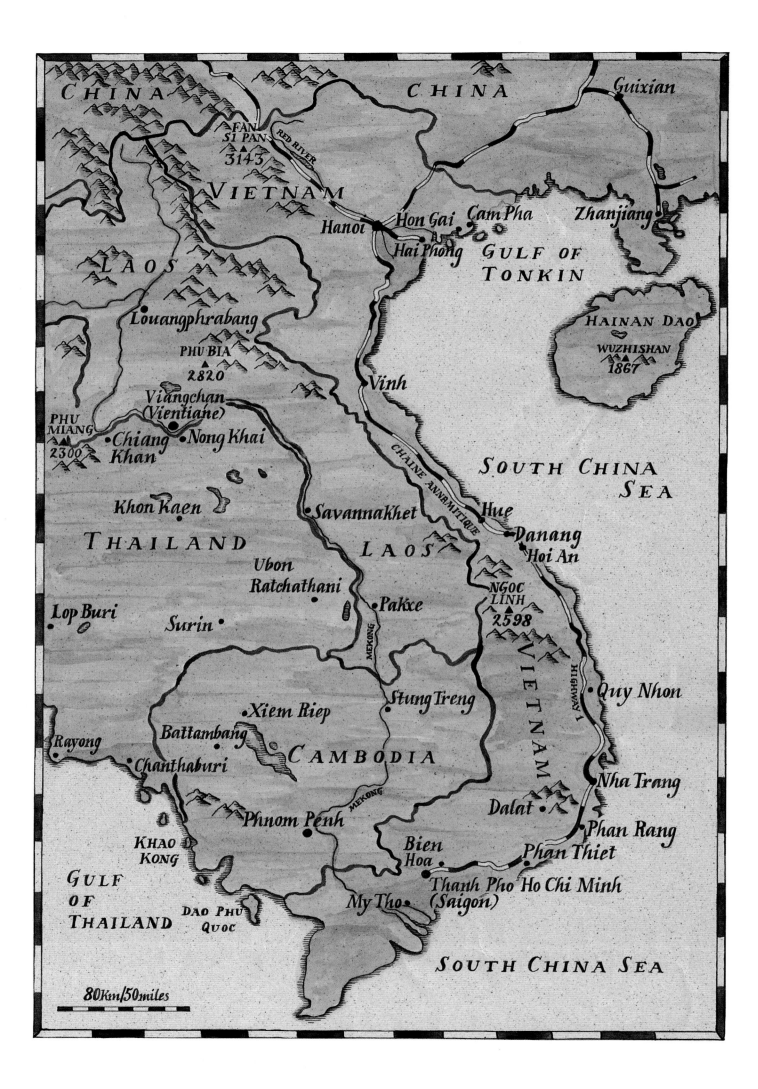

F O R E W O R D

It is an autumn morning in Hanoi. My Belgian friend and I sip a cup of lotus tea and enjoy the sight of emerald leaves quivering in the golden light. We talk about "Vietnamitude". I don't like the word. It smacks of colonization; worse, it rhymes with "servitude". Since one is free to create neologisms, we agree to use "Vietnamity", the Vietnamese identity. But that is not the problem. The problem comes when my friend suddenly asks, "What do you think is the essential characteristic of 'Vietnamity'?" It is a tough question.

I consider the work of two distinguished Vietnamologists, Huard and Durand, which highlights the Vietnamese concern not to assimilate foreign culture without first stamping it with their personal touch. It is an opinion which echoes that of Claude Palazzoli, a Hanoi expert, who believes that the originality of the Vietnamese attitude lies in its ability to incorporate foreign influences by cleverly modifying and adapting them so that the essential features of Vietnamese culture remain unaffected.

The "personal touch" and "essential features" mentioned by Huard, Durand and Palazzoli are the expressions of a Vietnamese identity which developed during the Bronze Age in the first millennium BC. It is important to underline this original Southeast Asian aspect which predates the influence of the Chinese culture.

In an interview, Hoang Xuan Han, a mathematician, sinologist and Vietnamologist, said: "Yes, there is a Vietnamese civilization. There is indeed a geographical area separate from the Chinese area, where an independent culture developed. In the mid-valley of the Yellow River, where the Chinese civilization started, bronze drums have never been found. Only tripods and quadripods (large urns with three or four legs), unknown in Vietnam, have been found there. One can cite other cultural aspects, too. The Vietnamese people of that era varnished their teeth, tattooed their bodies, chewed betel leaves; all customs which did not apparently exist in the northern part of the Yangtse Kiang."

These "other aspects", several of which were common to the first population of Southeast Asia, constitute the essence of the Vietnamese identity. This culture base was preserved despite ten centuries of Chinese domination.

Contact with a more sophisticated civilization, even one of invaders, prompted a feeling of both attraction and repulsion. Even while absorbing Chinese culture, the Viet believed in the fundamental importance of their own origins and customs.

Huu Ngoc

Historical Setting

Women of Saigon dressed in ao dai and elaborately embroidered slippers, c. 1900.

LAND OF MYTH AND LEGEND

There was once a beautiful princess, Au Co, wife of Lac Long Quan, King of the Dragons. His father was King of the Land of the Red Demons, while she was a descendant of the Immortals of the High Mountains. Au Co gave birth to a pouch containing a hundred eggs, which produced a hundred children. They were the first Vietnamese. Although they loved each other, the king and the princess knew that their origins were incompatible and they decided to part. Half the children followed their mother to the mountains, the rest left with their father for the lowlands. So the legend goes.

Like most legends, it reflects dreams and desires, nostalgia and hope. Few peoples have struggled as hard as the Vietnamese to preserve their national unity and to protect or recover their independence. It is as if they indeed were born of the same mother, as if the children of the mountains and those of the plains are expressing their longing to reunite.

One of the first kingdoms mentioned in the *Imperial Annals*, a poetic account of Vietnam's history, was the Van Lang, which came into existence some time between 1000 and 500 BC. It probably included most of today's north and part of central Vietnam. In 208 BC, Trieu Da, the governor of a province in southern China, enlarged his territory and proclaimed himself emperor of the new country, Nam Viet. Trieu Da reigned under the name of Vo Vuong and adopted the customs of the Viets. The nation was divided into two large provinces: what would later become Tonkin, and the northern part of the central region of Annam.

This inauguration scene was featured in Le Souvenir Indochinois, *published in Paris in 1932.*

Less than a century later, in 111 BC, the Chinese took control, and placed Nam Viet under the rule of the Han dynasty. It was the beginning of a thousand years of Chinese domination and of Vietnam's long, tenacious struggle against the Middle Kingdom. Vietnam's history is that of a people fascinated by Chinese traditions and culture, yet determined to keep their own cultural integrity. It is also the history of a dynamic, courageous and ambitious people, in search of new territories, of a new frontier. Vietnam as we know it today came into existence only in the 19th century, when in 1840 the Nguyen dynasty finally established sovereignty over the region of Soc Trang, in the southernmost tip of what was then known as Cochinchina.

China's control was constantly challenged. In most cities and towns of present-day Vietnam, there is a street dedicated to the "Two Ladies Trung" (Hai Ba Trung). The Trung sisters, fearless women of aristocratic background, led a celebrated revolt against the Middle Kingdom in AD 39–43. For a brief period, Trung Trac, whose husband had been killed by the Chinese, became "queen" of a territory called Giao Chi, which reached as far south as Hue. When Chinese troops defeated the Vietnamese two years later, the sisters committed suicide.

Following the Trung sisters' revolt, China imposed much tighter control over the occupied territory. Vietnam's culture, laws, written language, religion and many rituals were imported from China. But Chinese domination of Vietnam, often very severe, also led finally to the creation of truly local dynasties. By the beginning of the 10th century, the Chinese Tang dynasty was in decline, and in 939 a Vietnamese general, Ngo Quyen, after routing the Chinese at the Bach Dang river (938) and defeating a collection of lesser local warlords, estab-

Like his predecessors, Emperor Khai Dinh was basically a puppet emperor, controlled by the French.

lished himself as the King of Vietnam. Ngo Quyen's rule was brief. In 968 his dynasty was overthrown by a warlord, Dinh Tien Hoang, who united the country and instituted a system of universal military conscription. An accomplished diplomat, Dinh Tien Hoang sent an embassy to China, acknowledging its sovereignty and agreeing to pay a triennial tribute to the Empire. But by and large, Vietnam was now fully independent. As one historian wrote, "the smaller dragon had at last become strong enough to refuse obedience to the bigger".

Under the Ly dynasty (1010–1225), Vietnam (called Dai Viet) extended its borders by annexing several provinces of Champa, an Indianized kingdom in the south and repelling the Khmer Empire, then at the height of its power. Once in a while, the Chinese launched military incursions into Dai Viet, but most were successfully repelled.

As China had imposed its culture on Vietnam, so did Vietnam on the Champa population. The move to colonize the south had started, but domestic unrest and dynastic rivalries enabled the Chinese Ming dynasty to regain full control over Vietnam, but only for a few years (1406–1427). No matter how brief, the domination by the Ming would never be forgotten. The country was plundered by its new masters, high taxes deprived the peasants of what little they had, and a radical attempt was made to erase the local culture. Only the Chinese language was taught in schools, and all Vietnamese forms of worship were forbidden.

Like the Trung sisters, Le Loi, an aristocrat and landowner, has a street named after him in most Vietnamese cities. With the help of Nguyen Trai, an intellectual and one of Vietnam's great military strategists, Le Loi defeated the Ming dynasty in 1427, after nearly a decade of revolt. Under the name of Le Thai To, he founded the celebrated Later Le dynasty, which was to last until 1788. Vietnam was once again independent. Le Loi sympathized with the people, denounced the excesses of members of the ruling class and insisted on strict discipline for his troops.

The 15th century is considered a period of glory for Vietnam. The country was prosperous, dotted with palaces, forts and pagodas. Mandarins and members of the court lived in luxury. Countless military expeditions expanded the territory in the south.

Le Petit Journal
SUPPLÉMENT ILLUSTRÉ

A HANOÏ
Revue passée par M. Doumer et l'empereur d'Annam

Foreigners began to pour in during the 16th century. Commercial settlements were established in central Vietnam first by the Portuguese, then by the Dutch, the British and the French. Catholic missionaries arrived along with the traders, the merchants and the generals. Christian zeal was mixed with greed, and many missionaries played an important role at the king's court. The most famous of these missionary-diplomats is probably the French bishop Alexandre de Rhodes who wrote several important books on Asia. But he is better known today for his contribution to the phonetic transcription of Vietnamese, romanizing the language and adding accents to indicate the tones.

Scene featuring French governor general Paul Doumer and the Emperor of Annam, 1902.

Relations between the kings and the European missionaries were uneasy. Many mandarins saw the new Christian doctrine as a serious challenge to their power, and as a threat to Vietnamese and Confucian values. In the 17th century, especially in the north, missionaries were persecuted and executed. Many fled Vietnam. Only the court of the Nguyen, in Hue, maintained amicable relations with foreign priests, and a few were employed as mathematicians or astronomers. Good relations with the foreign missionaries were also used by various kings to obtain weapons and gunpowder. The Nguyen lords' successful resistance of the more powerful northern dynasty of the Trinh shogunate lords is largely due to the guns they procured from the Portuguese.

The feudal character of Vietnamese society, the conservatism of the mandarins and the bureaucrats, and the constant demands made on the peasants through taxes and conscription led to several popular uprisings during the 17th and 18th centuries. The most successful of these revolts is known as the Tay Son rebellion, conducted by three brothers from the village of Tay Son. By 1778, the Tay Son controlled Gia Dinh, the future Saigon-Cochinchina. The Tay Son soon overcame the weakening Trinh dynasty and provisorily maintained the Le dynasty. The brothers shared the country, installing themselves as kings of the north, the centre and the south. Although they paid tribute to the Le emperor, the monarch did not trust these rebels and fled to China. But the Tay Son were widely popular. One brother routed a powerful Chinese army of more than 200,000 soldiers with half as many men.

Under the name of Quang Trung, the second brother, from his new capital of Phu Xuan near Hue, tried to revive a country devastated by constant wars and internal conflicts. He is considered today as one of the greatest kings of Vietnam. Quang Trung died without a clear successor, and Nguyen Anh, the nephew of the Nguyen rulers, with the help of French advisers, took back Gia Dinh-Saigon, then Phu Xuan in 1801. Thang Long (the future Hanoi) was captured a few months later.

After a lengthy sojourn in France, the last emperor of the Nguyen dynasty, Bao Dai, takes his throne.

To symbolize the country's new unity, Nguyen Anh took the name Gia Long (from *Gia* Dinh and Thang *Long*, the southern and northern capitals). He changed the name of the country from Dai Viet to Nam Viet, although the Chinese decided it should be called Viet Nam. The new capital, Hue, was in the geographical centre of the nation.

Gia Long was an autocrat who followed closely the Chinese code of law. Resistance to the absolute power of the king and his government was treated as a most serious crime. He went as far as to forbid any religion not in favour of Confucianism and he imposed new taxes on the peasants, who already provided the bulk of the imperial army. He also got rid of traditional codes which specifically protected the status of women. In order to strengthen control by the central government, Gia Long decided to construct the Mandarin Road, linking the cities of Saigon, Hue and Hanoi. During his reign, important work was accomplished in the Mekong Delta, where large canals were dug. Foreign commerce became a state monopoly, with Chinese and Western traders the main beneficiaries. Gia Long's son, Minh Mang, continued to impose the same rigid Confucianism and reintroduced the Chinese alphabet. He proved more hostile than his father towards Western traders and priests.

In the 18th century, influential Bishop Pigneau de Behaine had been a fervent advocate of French involvement in Vietnam, actively patronizing

Nguyen Anh against the Tay Son rebels. The growing opposition of Gia Long's successors to French interests in Vietnam further encouraged France to revise its role in the region, and ultimately led to the subjugation of this proud nation by a Western colonial power.

France sent a military expedition against King Thieu Tri in Danang (a port the French called Tourane) in 1847. Twelve years later, Saigon was captured, and by 1867 the whole Mekong Delta was under French domination. The colony of Cochinchina had already been created in 1862, when Emperor Tu Duc signed the Treaty of Saigon. Tu Duc accepted not only the cession to France of three provinces in the south, but even agreed that Vietnam would pay a substantial sum to France for its losses in invading the country. The execution of Christians in the north by Tu Duc's troops gave France another excuse for large-scale intervention. The local Christians, Paris insisted, had to be protected. But, as one American commentator noted, "military and economic interests soon became the primary reason for remaining there".

Hanoi street scene depicted by Le Thanh Duc.

From their southern bases, French ships and troops pushed towards Annam and Tonkin. Cochinchina (South Vietnam) came under complete French control in 1867, but the French military conquest of Vietnam took time. In Hanoi, anti-French opposition was conducted with the unlikely assistance of an army of Chinese mercenaries, the famous Black Flag forces, who helped repel attempts to take Hanoi's Citadel in 1882. A few months after Tu Duc's death, in 1883, a Treaty of Protectorate was signed, marking the formal end of Vietnam's independence. The country was divided into three political entities: Tonkin, Annam and Cochinchina.

If many scholar-officials and most of the population continued to resist French domination, it was none the less welcomed by the Catholic minority, and by at least some Vietnamese who were convinced that the brutal, oppressive Tu Duc had lost "his heavenly mandate to rule".

The establishment in 1887 of the Indochinese Union (Vietnam, Laos and Cambodia) gave the French a vast stronghold in Asia. Cochinchina became a colony; Annam, Tonkin, Laos and Cambodia protectorates. The bulk of the country's bureaucracy, however, refused to serve the French. Paris, in turn, sent thousands of cadres and minor officials to Indochina.

Although France provided the country with schools and hospitals, and many French intellectuals and researchers took a genuine interest in Vietnamese culture, the colonizer also extracted a vast fortune from the soil, the forests and the sea. Taxes were heavy, and human exploitation, especially in the rubber plantations, was outrageous. But the resistance never gave up. The University of Hanoi, founded by the French, was closed for ten years in 1908, only a few months after it opened, because of anti-French activities.

Scholars such as Phan Boi Chau and Phan Chu Trinh, partly inspired by the example of modern Chinese leaders like Sun Yat-sen, founded nationalist movements which challenged French rule. Even the 16-year-old king, Duy Tan, left his palace in 1916 to join a revolt of Vietnamese troops. The king was arrested by the French and ended his life in exile on the distant island of Réunion.

The most important figure of the anti-colonial resistance is, of course, Nguyen That Thanh, better known as Ho Chi Minh. Born in 1890, he founded the Vietnam Youth League in 1925, the first Marxist organization in the country. In France, where he lived from 1911 to 1922, he published a newspaper, the *Pariah*, and joined the Communist Party. After being trained by the Soviets, he went to China to assist the revolution.

Portrait of Ho Chi Minh.

Ho Chi Minh's book, *Duong Cach Menh* (Revolutionary Path), published in 1926, voiced his conviction that the liberation of Asia from its colonial fate would come through the practice of Marxist-Leninism. The Communist Party was officially created on 17 June 1929 in Hanoi. During a meeting in Hong Kong on 3–7 February 1930, rival factions of the Party were formally united into a single organization. What Ho Chi Minh did until 1941, and where he was, is still a matter of controversy. Uncle Ho, as most Vietnamese call him, was a nationalist, a realist but also a poet, a humanist who usually advocated a more humane form of communism than many of his followers.

The history of anti-colonial resistance in Vietnam is more complex than orthodox Communist history would have us believe. But there is no doubt that Ho Chi Minh's talent for organization, and the Communist Party's strict discipline and ability to effectively channel popular anger to achieve concrete goals, played a decisive role in the victory over colonial power.

The occupation of Indochina by Japanese troops during World War II had demonstrated the fragility of the Western domination over Southeast Asia in general, and over Vietnam in particular. During the war, Ho Chi Minh appealed to all Vietnamese patriots to join his Communist-controlled League for the Independence of Vietnam (Vietnam Doc Lap Dong Minh Hoi). Among his supporters were Americans from the OSS, the precursor of the CIA, who appreciated his anti-Japanese stance. On 2 September 1945, in front of more than half a million people on Ba Dinh Square in Hanoi, Ho Chi Minh read the Vietnamese Declaration of Independence. It took another war, however — against France, this time — for Vietnam to gain its full independence. It ended with the French debacle of Dien Bien Phu, leading to the signing of the Geneva Agreement in 1954. Vietnam had finally regained its freedom, yet it was still a divided country.

The reunification of the country became a priority of the Communist Party, by now in power in the north. But conditions were not ripe, as the new Democratic Republic of Vietnam was struggling with economic and social

problems. The National Liberation Front of South Vietnam, founded in December 1960, provided the Communist leadership with a large front to direct the fighting against the southern republic and its American allies, without being the obvious leaders of the conflict.

Artist's rendition of a poultry vendor.

Increased American military assistance was unable to prevent the southern regime's collapse in 1975. Many people in the south saw the fight against the American-backed administration as a nationalist struggle. They rejoiced in the liberation of 1975, but soon realized they had little appetite for the austere brand of communism that was soon imposed on them. Thousands fled by boat in the late 1970s and early 1980s, claiming that Vietnam, now called the Socialist Republic of Vietnam, was not Vietnam anymore, that centuries-old traditions had been abandoned or forbidden. The Communist Party had won the war, but it was about to lose the peace.

At its 1986 congress, however, the Communist Party called for liberalization of the economy and a revival of Vietnam's traditional culture. It was the beginning of a vast change that still continues. The transformation from the rigid, dogmatic regime was dramatic. By 1992, Vietnam was a bustling, developing nation, a major exporter of rice and a drawcard for foreign investors. The policy of liberalization also brought about a revival of Vietnam's glorious past in the form of artistic and literary freedom.

The traditional remedy of cupping (above): a small glass cup is heated and placed on the skin, creating a temporary vacuum to draw out "bad wind".

Following pages: High-ranking mandarins wearing ceremonial dress, Hue, 1927 (left).

Plucking poultry in Cholon, 1900 (top right).

Seated on a high wooden platform, a 19th-century Annamese family shares a meal (right).

The Land

Industrious and hard-working seem feeble descriptions when applied to the Vietnamese people. Some 75 percent of the work force toils in the fields, using means of cultivation that have stood them in good stead for centuries. Here, a farmer and his water buffalo carve fields into a neat patchwork.

THE VIETNAMESE SOUL

They fought the Chinese, the Khmers, the Cham, the Japanese, the French, the Americans. And since time immemorial, the Vietnamese have struggled with the destructiveness of nature. Typhoons devastate the coastal areas with deadly regularity; and the Red River, great and tumultuous provider of northern Vietnam's prosperity, is as much a blessing as a seasonal threat. The northern delta region, the most densely populated of the country, is never more than 3 metres above sea level.

A complex network of dikes and canals have for centuries tried to regulate the flows, while allowing for irrigation of the rice fields. It is a clever but frail system. Every year during the rainy season, thousands of people living along the river in the suburbs of Hanoi are forced by the rising waters to abandon their homes and move their modest belongings to makeshift shelters around the old French district of the capital.

Vietnam, a tropical country of lowlands, hills, mountains and forests, is an elongated "S" in shape, 1,650 kilometres long but only 50 kilometres wide at the centre. The two deltas, the Red River in the north and the Mekong in the sub-tropical south, are the rice bowls of a fast-growing population. With the general liberalization of the economy, farmers have regained ownership of their land and production has increased dramatically. Vietnam has become the third largest exporter of rice in the world.

The head monk of Chua Quan The An, a monastery nestled amongst the Marble Mountains outside Danang.

The central region has large but diminishing forests, volcanic basalt soil, and profitable tea and coffee plantations. The highlands, the home of many of the country's minority groups, are cooler. The Mekong is one of the great rivers of the world. Born in Tibet, it fertilizes China, Burma, Laos, Thailand and Cambodia before forming the fertile southern delta of Vietnam. This delta, one of the best rice-growing areas in the world, is home to half the southern population. Rich alluvial deposits accumulate at the mouth of the river, extending the coastline of Vietnam by 75 metres every year.

With close to 70 million inhabitants and a total surface of 331,688 square kilometres, Vietnam borders China to the north, Laos and Cambodia to the west, and the Pacific Ocean to the east and the south. It divides naturally into three main regions: Bac Bo (north), Trung Bo (centre) and Nam Bo (south), known to the French as Tonkin, Annam and Cochinchina.

Seasons are regulated by the monsoon. From November to early April, monsoon winds blow from the Chinese coast, and the weather is relatively cool, especially in the north. The summer monsoon brings hot air from the Gobi Desert, accompanied by heavy rainfall.

Vietnam is dominated by the Viet (or Kinh) ethnic group, which represents more than 88 percent of the total population. They coexist with more than 50 other nationalities, from Khmer to Chinese (or Hoa), from Thai to Hmong. A great number of these ethnic groups, with the obvious exception of the Chinese, live in the central highlands or the northern border areas. Minorities have their own culture, much of which has survived, and at least 11 groups — the Tay, Thai, Nung, Hmong, Muong, Cham, Khmer, Ede, Bahnar and Jarai — have their own writing systems. The fiercely independent Ede, Bahnar and Jarai were named Moi (a somewhat pejorative term, meaning "savage") by the Vietnamese. The French, more elegantly, called them Montagnards.

The early Viets in the Red River Delta (1st millennium BC) quickly developed their own strong cultural identity, an identity that was forged and refined through centuries of foreign invasions and wars.

Typical farming landscape in central Quang Nam province.

Ancient Vietnamese society was dominated by the king, who was served by mandarins and nobles. Below were the intellectuals, peasants, artisans, merchants and, at the bottom of the ladder, soldiers. As in China, the strong influence of Confucianism helped maintain feudal social structures. Confucianism is based on the five essential relationships, subordinations that structure the entire society: subjects to rulers, sons to fathers, wives to husbands, younger brothers to older brothers and respect between friends. But before the introduction of Confucius's ideals, Vietnam had developed its own particular identity, a mixture of animism, ancestor worship and even what has been described as a form of matriarchal society. This is seen in legends, and is illustrated by a number of famous heroines found in the history of Vietnam. Many of them were warriors, from Ba Trieu to Bui Thi Xuan or more recently Nguyen Thi Binh, who was a deputy commander-in-chief of the National Liberation Front.

The influence of the matriarchal system has probably survived better among some of the minority populations, where it is not unusual to have a woman as head of the village. Muong leaders, for instance, are said to have as many as five husbands.

The 18th-century novel-poem of Nguyen Du, the *Kieu*, is one of the most celebrated illustrations of the complexity of the Vietnamese culture; of the constant struggle between the ideals and wishes of the individual and the pressure to conform to strict Confucian norms; between the desire for individual freedom and respect for established law and order. A writer and specialist on popular culture, Huu Ngoc, sees the *Kieu*, more than any other text, as representing the "Vietnamitude", or Vietnamese national character. Rarely has a literary work been so popular, known by both intellectuals and peasants, and read constantly since the day of its publication. The two main heroes, Kieu herself, the beautiful heroine, and Tu Hai, the rebel who defies the power of the king, are especially dear to readers. Kieu falls in love with a young scholar, but later decides to raise money to help free her falsely accused and imprisoned father by offering herself as a concubine to a rich merchant. The 3,000 verses of the novel-poem narrate with unusual realism

and great lyricism the constant inner conflict between love and duty endured by Kieu.

It is a conflict every Vietnamese can identify with. The *Kieu* is in many ways an indictment of feudalism, but it also challenges what Huu Ngoc calls the "sacrosanct notion of fidelity according to which a woman must devote her life to a single man, even after his death". Nguyen Du's masterpiece goes against the puritanism of Confucianism when he makes precise allusion to "the jade and ivory beauty" of Kieu. In Vietnam, the people "fall in love early, have sexual relations early, get married early". Kieu both revolts against and consents to this puritanism.

Flecks of gold paint sparkle on Hue's Palace of Supreme Harmony, Tien Thai Hoa, in the Citadel.

The history of Vietnam is marked by a series of popular revolts against powerful leaders who had lost "their mandate from heaven". Vietnamese literature is full of references to the power of the people. As one Ca Dao (popular poem-song) explains:

> *The Mandarins pass*
> *But the people will endure forever*
> *The inscriptions on stone stelae wear out*
>   *after one hundred years,*
> *But the people's judgment is not forgotten*
>   *after one thousand years.*

The Chinese were in Vietnam for more than a thousand years, the French for over a century and a half. Both civilizations left a deep imprint, but they failed completely to eradicate the country's national character. Confucianism's rigidity was always challenged by the rebellious nature of the commoners. The village and the family remained the focal point of a citizen's life, and the traditional Vietnamese village is the centre of a complex network of social relations in which everybody has a well-defined role. But the village was never a docile structure. There is a famous Vietnamese saying proclaiming that "the power of the emperor stops at the gate of the village". This is as true today as it was centuries ago.

Even the casual visitor to Vietnam will notice the quality of the handicrafts, the richness of artistic expression. Some villages specialize in a specific craft. Not far from Hanoi, the town of Tranh Lang Ho, in Bach Ninh province, has been carving printing blocks and producing folk print paintings for centuries. Inlaid mother-of-pearl on furniture is an especially important craft and has been traced to the reign of Le Hien Ton and Gia Long in the 19th century. Lacquer came from China in the 15th century and was at first considered a craft, using a limited range of colours — red, gold, brown and black. French-educated artists later introduced the Western concept of the artist as a creator, and lacquer, with new colours and new subjects, began to appear in the exhibition halls.

Massive Buddha statues have been carved in the cave-shrine of the Marble Mountains.

The capacity of Vietnam to assimilate foreign influence without losing its own soul is also reflected in the variety of local religions. The vast majority of Vietnamese are Buddhist, followers of a Buddhism that tolerates in its pagodas many deities of Chinese or animist origins. Catholicism is the faith of more than 6 million people. But several indigenous religions have appeared in the course of the centuries. These usually derived from Buddhism, as in the case of the Hoa Hao, founded in 1919 by the "Crazy Monk", Huynh Phu So. He took an extremely puritanical view of Buddhism, urging his followers to get rid of the pagodas and the clergy, banning alcohol, opium and gambling. The new religion, called Phat Giao Hoa Hao, or Purified Buddhism of Hoa Hao, became popular in the southern delta. During World War II, the sect raised an army with the assistance of the Japanese. Afterwards, the Hoa Hao became a conservative political party and lost much of its influence.

Better known and still very much alive today, Cao Daism was founded in the 1920s. It is also a reformed Buddhism with some Taoist, Confucianist and Christian overtones. The founder of Cao Daism, Ngo Van Chieu, was a minor bureaucrat in the French colonial machinery. He claimed that he received a message from a superior spirit in 1919, urging him to look harder for the way to illumination. The spirit returned two years later, claimed he was Cao Dai, the "High Terrace", the Supreme Being, and told Ngo Van Chieu to start a new synchretic religion. Ngo Van Chieu tried indeed to unite all the religions existing in Vietnam into one single faith. Cao Dai is the emanation of Buddha and Jesus Christ. In Cao Dai temples, Buddha and Jesus are joined in the Pantheon by Lao Tse, Quan An, Victor Hugo, Joan of Arc, Sun Yat Sen, the French astronomer Flammarion, Louis Pasteur or, more recently, Winston Churchill. The religion was officially formed in 1925, on Christmas night, when Vietnamese officials, many of them colleagues of

A woman carries a carefully balanced load of hay across the bridge in Hoi An (left).

Row upon strict row of cabbages (right). A growing population combined with the damage wrought by decades of conflict and virtually unrestricted logging has drastically reduced the amount of forested land: great tracts of forest covered 44 percent of Vietnam in 1944; by 1991 that figure had dropped below 25 percent. But since 1987, a National Conservation Strategy has implemented tree-planting programmes and set up reserves and national parks.

Ngo Van Chieu, gathered to hear yet another message from Cao Dai. The first pope of the new church was Le Van Trung, the founder having declined the honour.

The followers of the church are divided into three groups. The Religious observe strict rules of vegetarianism, chastity and simplicity, while the Faithful just obey the rules of the religion. In between are the Mediums, a group of 12 wise people who receive messages from the high spirits. Their existence reflects Nguyen Van Chieu's fascination with spiritualism and the occult. Although Cao Daism was recognized as an official religion by the French colonial power, the Cao Dai, like the Hoa Hao, received weapons from the Japanese during World War II. Pham Cong Tac, the successor of Le Van Trung, was arrested by the French for alleged contacts with a Vietnamese prince in exile in Japan. He was liberated in 1946 and it was the turn of the French to arm the Cao Dai, hoping they would fight the Viet Minh. The Cao Dai then clashed with Ngo Dinh Diem in the mid-1950s, and Pope Pham Cong Tac fled to Cambodia. A new twist came a few years later, when the Americans persuaded the Cao Dai to fight communism alongside President Diem. To this day, the Cao Dai retain deep religious influence in the south. The main Cao Dai cathedral, built in 1927 in Long Than, is an impressive structure, dominated by the Eye of Cao Dai, the main symbol of the church, a sign of clairvoyance, which seems to float above the majestic altar.

The temperate climate and near-constant sunshine which blesses Dalat provides ideal conditions for growing tobacco in the hills of Lam Dong province (top). Women wield crude scoops to irrigate paddy fields (above).

Latex trickles down the tapped-out spirals of a rubber tree near Vung Tao (left). Introduced by the French, rubber was the second most lucrative export during the 19th century. But the industry's history is a harsh one, built on the backs of indentured labourers who endured a miserable existence.

The cultivation of Vietnam's primary crop is usually carried out by women (above). A labyrinth of tributaries fuels the rich Mekong Delta with precious water and fertile soil. Seedlings are transplanted in the lush fields of "green gold" encircling Hoi An (right).

After the harvest comes threshing (above) and sieving of the rice (right). With threshing equipment by no means common, farmers often draw on unsuspecting vehicles to separate the rice from the stalk. Piles of rice stalks are regularly seen on roads in the Red and Mekong deltas, as are rice, corn and other vegetables drying alongside.

A rare moment of calm on Nha Trang's municipal beach, before the usual incursion of Vietnamese families who enjoy a regular early morning bathe (following pages).

The fishing fleets around Nha Trang tend to set out at night. Daylight hours are spent preparing the vessels, weaving and repairing nets. The catch may include lobster, abalone, shrimps, snapper, tuna or cuttlefish.

Nets are carefully stored in a basket boat (hung chai) for transport to a fishing trawler. Made of woven bamboo strips and liberally daubed with pitch to make them waterproof, the boats are rowed standing up, with a single oar.

The floating community of Tai An leads a quiet existence, ordered by the tide's ceaseless ebb and flow (following pages).

Hon Ba Temple, set on a tiny island near the tip of Vung Tao, attracts devotees and the curious (above). The temple may be reached on foot at low tide.

Surf rolls up on Bai Sau, or Back Beach, an eight-kilometre stretch along the southeastern side of the Vung Tao peninsula (left). Known as Cap Saint Jacques by the French, this triangle-shaped resort has been frequented by residents of Saigon since the 1890s, by virtue of its proximity to the city. Originally the customs and immigration centre for Saigon, Vung Tao gained notoriety in recent years for the number of refugees who began their flight from its shores.

In Cam Ranh Bay, intense heat evaporates sea water which has been diverted to shallow channels, leaving behind thick grains of salt. Workers, well protected against the sun's harsh rays, rake the salt for further drying, then fill baskets hung from shoulder poles to carry it to what resembles a snow-capped peak.

Rice is bagged and stacked, ready for export (following pages).

Imposing remnants of the ancient Champa civilization dot the countryside around Danang. Formed in the 2nd century AD, the kingdom of this Hindu-influenced people extended from Hai Van Pass (Annam Gate) in what is now central Vietnam to Vung Tau in the south. Temples, such as those found around the southern city of Phan Rang (left), were intended only for the use of the nobility. Situated on a slight rise on the outskirts of Nha Trang, the temple complex of Po Nagar (above) was the Cham's main spiritual centre in the south.

Nestled amongst the greenery at the foot of the Marble Mountains outside Danang, near the Trang Thien Pagoda, is a monastery and temple (following pages).

The People

Soft morning sunlight filters into Vinh Nghiem Pagoda in Ho Chi Minh City.

Shanty-town dweller in Ho Chi Minh City (top left). Grocery merchant in Haiphong (top right). Composer Van Cao wrote Vietnam's national anthem (above left). One of the local keepers of Hoi An's Assembly of the Quang Dong Chinese Congregation (above right).

Faded diplomas, old photographs and carvings are silent yet eloquent testimony to Hanoi historian Dr Le Van Khoi's passion for the past (right).

The sandwich vendor's wares typically consist of crusty baguettes, chicken, pâté, fish or pork, onions and vegetables, with tasty condiments of chilli and ginger (above).

A woman shades herself from the scorching sun against a backdrop of pomelos (right).

Two staples of Vietnamese cuisine: the glossy chilli pepper (top), its burnished sheen hinting at the fire lurking inside, and French bread (above), made with wheat flour in the north and rice flour in the south.

In the courtyard of a Cholon noodle shop, bundles of the tightly twisted strands are packed into baskets (top). A profusion of fresh vegetables at a Dalat market stall includes pumpkins, cucumbers, tomatoes and mushrooms (above).

Some 60 different hilltribes are scattered among the Hoang Lien mountains of the north and the Annamite Cordillera, which stretches along central Vietnam's borders with Cambodia and Laos. Tribal villages can be found on the lofty plateau near Ban Me Thout (right). The Black Tai belong to the country's largest ethnic minority group. Cups of strong tea, and even stronger tobacco, are customary when entertaining guests or visitors (above).

The Brau (left) worship a sky genie. They live an almost nomadic life, due to their slash-and-burn farming methods. Women of the Bru Van Kieu minority carry hand-woven baskets of goods to market (top). Their teeth are stained black from betel-nut chewing. A child of the Black Thai minority (above) who live in the north, between the Black and Red rivers.

One of the most tragic legacies of the Vietnam war, Amerasian children, like these boys (above) in Ho Chi Minh City, face intolerance and rejection in the land of their birth as well as the country of their fathers.

Dubbed "Montagnards", or highlanders, by the French, Vietnam's hilltribe groups live mainly in the northern mountains and Central Highlands. A woman and her grandson (right), on a Sunday visit to Dalat, display the generation gap which exists in minority groups.

Organized chaos in a Ho Chi Minh City schoolyard (following pages). The thirst for education runs deep in Vietnamese children, especially the desire to become conversant in English. Their grandparents may speak French, but English is now perceived as a more effective passport to success.

Students study English at a former private Chinese school in Hanoi (above). Until this century, the traditional Chinese mandarinal system of education was followed. Although elementary and then secondary schools were instituted by the French, the literacy rate remained exceptionally low. Expanding educational horizons was an important goal of the revolution. Now, schooling in Vietnam is compulsory and free. The literacy rate of between 85 percent and 95 percent is one of the highest in Asia.

Kitted out in traditional kung fu uniform, a boy in Hanoi takes a break (left).

A martial arts master in Ho Chi Minh City tests his young pupils' technique (above). The study of such pastimes is limited, as most young people spend their free hours working to contribute to the family income.

A young woman in Ho Chi Minh City peers out from beneath the brim of her stylish straw hat (right). The traditional ao dai is making something of a comeback — the high-necked, full-length tunic slit to the waist and worn over long, loose trousers is at once practical and captivating.

Pairs of new shoes tacked to a crumbling wall in Hanoi's Old Quarter are the equivalent of a window display for this shoemaker. Throughout Vietnam, commercial transactions are not always handled within regimented spaces like shops or offices; goods are manufactured, repaired and traded, their relative merits and defects debated and considered in a jumble of business that spills out to cover sidewalks and street corners.

Clear skies and an accommodating tree trunk on which to place his mirror are the only conditions this barber requires. He and many colleagues do a brisk business in the old French Quarter of Hanoi, Hoan Kiem.

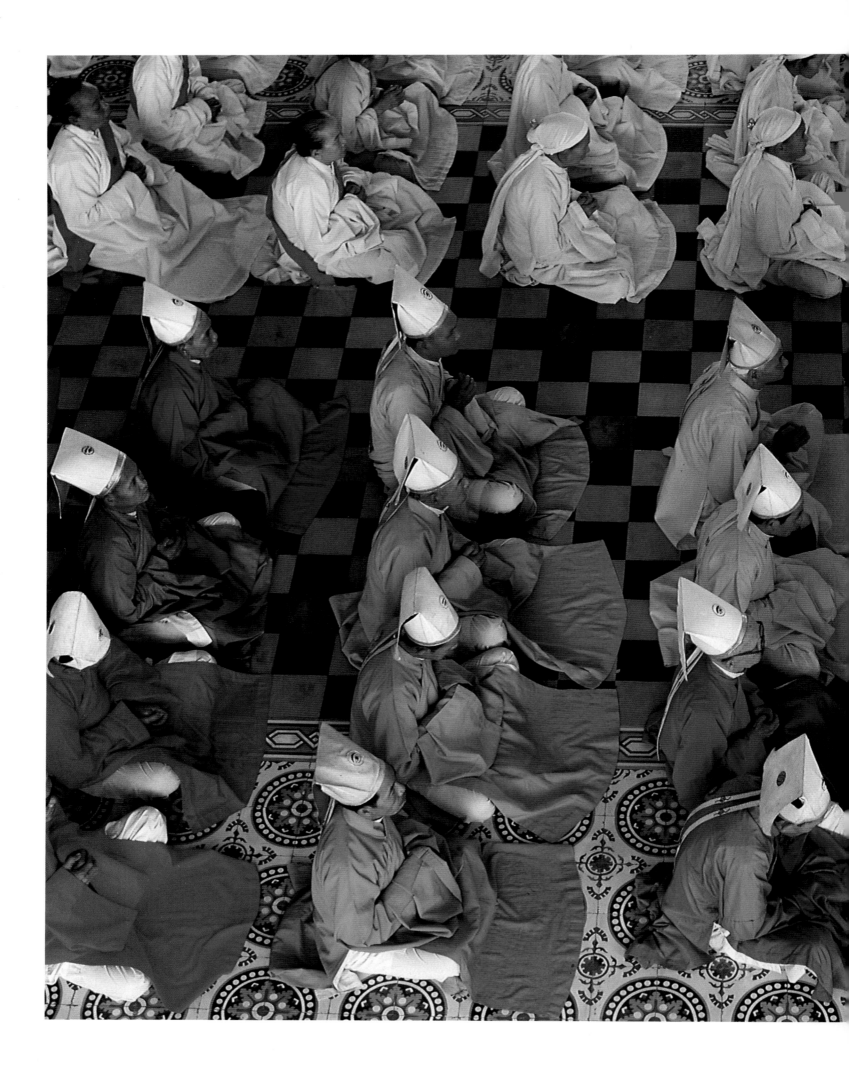

Traditions

Indigenous to Vietnam, Cao Daism is surely one of the country's most fascinating extant religions. Seances, such as those in which founder Ngo Van Chieu received messages from Cao Dai in the early 1920s, are conducted regularly. Every aspect of Cao Daism reflects its fusion of Eastern and Western philosophies — secular and religious.

Four ceremonies punctuate the day at Cao Dai temples (left). Female priests worship on the left, male priests on the right. The Great Temple at the Holy See in Tay Ninh (above) is a rich panoply of extremes of French and Chinese architecture. The "divine eye" floats above every altar.

The all-seeing eye also appears above the portico of the Great Temple (above). It became the religion's symbol after appearing in a vision to Ngo Van Chieu.

Chinese characters on the window of a Cao Dai temple exhort followers to do good deeds (right).

Monks in Ho Chi Minh City (left). While the majority of Vietnamese are of the Buddhist faith, their Buddhism is distinctive in that it has over the centuries incorporated aspects of Confucianism, Taoism and animism. A ceremony is held at the Pho Minh Pagoda (above) in Rach Gia. The Buddha was the gift of a Buddhist organization in Thailand.

A door guardian, gracing the entrance to a temple in Hanoi, glowers fiercely from his post (following pages). Detail of his intricately decorated robe indicates a costume as fearsome as his expression.

A golden dragon, symbol of nobility and power, snakes around a doorway of the Temple of Literature in Hanoi (above). Here, in 1076, Vietnam's first university was established, intended solely for the sons of mandarins.

Perfumed smoke from joss sticks swirls in the air of the Emperor of Jade Pagoda, in Ho Chi Minh City (right). The temple was built by the Canton Congregation early this century.

Garbed in white — the traditional colour of mourning — bereaved family members and friends accompany the deceased in a funeral procession on Phu Quoc Island (following pages).

A lone monk sits before the golden Buddha at Vinh Nghiem Pagoda, the largest pagoda in Ho Chi Minh City. The temple complex includes an eight-storey tower in which there is a Buddha at each level, and a three-storey repository for funerary urns.

Backstage, Thu Do Theatre in Cholon, actors begin a lengthy make-up session that will transform them into easily recognizable characters. Despite obvious Chinese influences, separate and uniquely Vietnamese theatrical art forms have evolved. The most recent development is Cai Luong, "Renovated Opera", which emerged in the 1920s, taking as its influence French comedies of the era.

An artist painstakingly copies a reproduction from an art volume (above). Copy painting doesn't carry the stigma it does in the West; rather, these artists view meticulously accurate copies as proof of their talent. It is also extremely lucrative.

A painter displays his self-portrait in Hanoi (left). It is not uncommon to see artists tucked away in a narrow street space, hunched over tiny black and white portraits, reproducing them faithfully.

Crimson is the colour of Tet: drums, firecrackers and holy men's robes are a rich red, hinting at the vitality of what is to come. At midnight on the first day of the first lunar month, an incredible din signals the start of the new year. Pounding drums and exploding firecrackers herald seven days of revelry.

Rituals and ceremonies are an integral part of life. A ceremony is held at the official opening of a new store in Cholon (left), the date of which is chosen carefully for its auspiciousness. During the shaman ritual of the Lemdong ceremony (above), the master enters a trance and absorbs the spirits of the dead. It is an intense and strange affair, with the priest wearing a succession of brilliantly coloured costumes and dancing energetically.

A study in reflection; a Buddhist monk studies scriptures. Mahayana Buddhism, literally "from the north", is the predominant religion of Vietnam. Mahayanists believe everyone has the potential to become a Bodhisattva; one who perfects himself or herself in the necessary virtues but elects to stay in this world to do good.

An aged nun at Tay Phuong Pagoda, west of Hanoi, bids a visitor welcome.

Hanoi

There is probably no better way to savour the intriguing mélange of stately colonial-era buildings, Buddhist pagodas, temples, lakes, tree-lined boulevards and twisted back alleys of Hanoi than by cyclo (from the French "cyclo-pousse"). Tourists enjoy availing themselves of a leisurely, non-polluting ride to such landmarks as the Ambassadors' Pagoda. Driver commentary is an optional extra.

AN ABIDING CHARM LIVES ON

The Hanoi I first knew, only a few years after the end of the Vietnam war, was a grey, subdued, crumbling, decrepit, quasi-silent city. And yet, it was dignified and fascinating, poor but with an indefinable charm. At dusk the streets were dark, as there were no public lights. Hanoi was like a ghost town with only a few people walking slowly, hesitantly, along deserted avenues, often a flashlight in hand to avoid falling into one of the numerous bomb craters that still dotted the sidewalks.

The Hanoi of today has retained much of its particular charm. But it is also a lively city, full of intense commercial activity, where new restaurants, hotels and offices appear almost daily. Explosions of colour have replaced the uniformity of the dull grey and green tones favoured during the years of dogmatic communism. It is still a city where bicycles and motorbikes have a greater presence than cars and trucks, although during rush hour Hanoi is experiencing its first-ever traffic jams.

In 1010, the founder of the new Ly dynasty, Ly Thai-Ton, moved the capital from Hoa Lu to the area occupied today by Hanoi. He called the site on the bank of the Red River, Thang Long, the Soaring Dragon. He built a new Citadel to replace the old Chinese fort, which had been abandoned for decades. Moving capital cities was not new. Many kings before Thai-Ton had done the same. There was no glory in maintaining old constructions nor prestige in preserving the past. A change of power needed new visible symbols. Yet Thang Long was to remain the capital of Vietnam for most of the following millennium because it was situated so close to the main route of communication, the majestic Red River which connects the centre of political power with both China and Vietnam's northern regions, including the beautiful border area, sugar-loaf mountains, and the tormented coastlines of Ha Long Bay.

Elaborate facades of Hanoi's Old Quarter provide storage and working areas for local tradespeople.

Early Thang Long was a modest town. The wall built by Thai-Ton covered a perimeter of approximately 4,700 metres. Inside was what the writer Georges Azambre described as a "small territory of rice fields, gardens, marshes" which eventually grew into a superb metropolis. The French writer Claude Farrère described the Hanoi of the early 1920s as "a magnificent capital, a metropolis of 150,000 inhabitants, white and green, with pleasant shadows, rich, very gracious, very voluptuous".

Hanoi today is basically an inner city of more than a million inhabitants, as many bicycles, half a million motorbikes, and a master plan to expand to the suburbs in order to retain, as much as possible, the historic character of the old town.

The fortified centre, called Long-Thanh, was originally reserved for the king, the court and high-ranking government officials. Access to the core of the town was strictly limited to the ruling class. The ordinary people — merchants, craftsmen, farmers and small bureaucrats — lived outside the walls. One had to wait for the 19th century to see this strict division be challenged, partly due to French influence.

The name "Hanoi" appeared only in 1831, and was initially that of an entire province. At the beginning there was not a single large capital but rather a collection of small villages near the Citadel, with their own bamboo gates and their own relative autonomy.

The hodge-podge of new concrete blocks and old-style courtyard houses of the Old Quarter.

At least one monument remains of the Ly dynasty, the famous Chua Mot Cot, or One Pillar Pagoda, not far from the Mausoleum of President Ho Chi Minh. Also known as the Temple of Love, the pagoda was first built in 1049, restored in the 1920s, burned by the retreating French in 1954 and renovated once again the following year. The original wooden pillar is now made of stone. The pagoda, shaped like a lotus emerging from the water, contains a statue of the Goddess of Mercy, Quan An. Emperor Ly Thai-Ton, childless for many years, built the pagoda to thank the goddess for a son his young peasant wife finally bore him. The emperor had dreamt that Quan An offered him a baby boy lying on a lotus leaf.

Little remains of the Royal Palace of the Le dynasty, destroyed in the 17th century, and which used to be at the centre of the Citadel. It was a tradition of new dynasties to abandon palaces built by their predecessors and to erect new royal residences nearby.

Urban development in the last 200 years has also taken its toll on historical edifices. The Citadel, built by the Nguyen dynasty in 1805, which comprised the famous flag tower near the Army museum, was simply razed at the end of the 19th century to make room for villas and new avenues. The present central post office replaced a beautiful pagoda.

The old commercial district, the Old Quarter, is located in the general direction of the rising sun (symbolic of the emergence and power of the king), east of the Citadel. It offers a maze of small streets, scenes of intense activity, which spread almost to the banks of the Red River. Each street is dedicated to a specific guild and bears the name of its speciality. There is a street for silk (Dao) and one for hats (Non); one for shoes (Giay) and one for rice (Xuan). The most fragrant are probably the fermented fish (Mam) and dyes (Tho Nhuom) streets.

Leisurely walks in the old district bring constant discoveries. Here you can buy flags, wooden cooking molds, traditional musical instruments, or even rubber stamps for printing your own ceremonial paper money. This is the Hanoi painted again and again by the most famous contemporary Vietnamese painter, Buy Xuan Phai, who lived at the centre of the old town

until his death in 1988, in the small house once inhabited by his father. Only a few years ago, his paintings were selling for just a few dollars. However, they have since been discovered by foreign collectors and now frequently fetch thousands of dollars.

A pipe seller demonstrates his wares.

Of course, even the Old Quarter has changed. A few of the 19th-century houses, with their curved roofs decorated with Chinese characters, remain. Most of them, however, date from early this century. They are simple structures, with a ground floor dedicated to business and an upper floor for family living. Thanh Quan, a 19th-century district officer and poet, celebrated the old city as the "Soul of Hanoi".

The area earned its revolutionary credentials in 1906, when the Dong Kinh Nghia Thuc movement, led by a few intrepid nationalist intellectuals, organized an uprising against the French. The rebels, to everybody's surprise, held on for more than two months against the armoured vehicles of General Leclerc before they managed to escape with their weapons and their wounded comrades along the riverbanks.

Hanoi is the cultural centre of Vietnam. As the writer To Hoai explains, Hue was a small city, the temporary capital of the Nguyen dynasty, and never became the true intellectual centre of Vietnam. Few intellectuals followed the Nguyen to Hue, choosing instead to remain in Hanoi. The Temple of Literature, Van Mieu, remained the most important focal point of mandarinal examination. Chinese ambassadors never went to Hue, only to Hanoi. The city of Saigon, or Ho Chi Minh City, is young and brash, dedicated to commerce rather than cultural activities. The School of Fine Arts and the Conservatory of Music in Hanoi have for decades set high standards. Even during the Vietnam war, the city's painters, musicians, actors and dancers were evacuated to the countryside and classes took place in trenches.

Numerous art galleries have opened in recent years along with shops boasting high-quality local handicrafts. In Hanoi, new novels, poems and films are discussed with all the intensity one could find in the old Parisian literary salons. Water puppet shows, unique to the north, are amazing in their naive and joyful vivacity.

Hanoi is still a city where people have time, and thanks to the more relaxed political atmosphere that fol-lowed the 6th Congress of the Commu-nist Party in December 1986, friends can again fully enjoy the art of conver-sation: neighbours are not afraid to visit each other. Few private houses have a telephone, so it is normal to just drop by unannounced. There will al-ways be a cup of tea, and often cakes or a glass of home-made medicinal alcohol for the unexpected guest.

Vendors sell a dream of riches beyond belief: lottery tickets.

With its combination of palaces and fortresses, some in ruins, its temples and pagodas, its vast avenues bor-dered by sumptuous villas and mansions, refreshing lakes and gardens, its old districts and more recent museums, Hanoi is a true architectural treasure. But it is never a pretentious city. Even the French Quarter has the quiet charm of a provincial Mediterranean town. Vestiges of ancient monuments do not overpower. As in Rome, they are just part of daily life.

While there is an urgent need to upgrade an infrastructure often dating back to the days of the French and planned for a population of no more than 200,000 people (Hanoi and its environs in 1992 had more than 2.5 million inhabitants), it is no less necessary to preserve the unique character of the Vietnamese capital. The entire city is a monument to the people of Vietnam and their traditions, a testimony to the uniqueness of the local culture, a living museum that should be guarded from erratic modernization and the greed of those more interested in making money than in preserving the glory of the past and the charm of the present.

The State Bank (right) and Presidential Palace (above): After 1883, when Hanoi became a French protectorate, many of the existing buildings were torn down. In their place rose a grand architectural style to which so much of the city's character is attributed.

Ho Chi Minh's body lies in an imposing marble mausoleum (top). The revolutionary leader is popularly referred to as "Uncle Ho". Across the square is the National Assembly Hall and Party Headquarters.

The Viet Minh flag (above) was raised for the first time at exactly 11 am on 9 October 1954, over the Palais du Gouvernement in Hanoi. It would be more than two decades before Ho Chi Minh's emblem flew over a unified Vietnam.

Ancient history is wonderfully tangible in Hanoi, and nowhere more so than in the pagodas. On an islet off the shore of West Lake is Tran Quoc Pagoda (above), where a stele dating from 1639 gives historical details of the site.

Upon its erection in the 11th century, the Van Mieu, or Temple of Literature (top right), was dedicated to Confucius. Within the compound is the Temple of the Military and the University of Literature and Ethics. Its original purpose — to educate future mandarins — was uncannily echoed by the French, who turned it into the Ecole National d'Administration. The entrance to Tran Quoc Pagoda (right), beside Ho Tay, West Lake.

A former general with the French regime (above), passing the time in a Hanoi barbershop, still displays traces of a military bearing.

Framed by the soft folds of ao dai, a tailor runs up another of the traditional outfits on his treadle sewing machine (right).

In the Old Quarter, also known as the 36 Streets (above), a pair of grandmothers keep watch over pre-school members of their families.

The waters of Hoan Kiem Lake glisten outside Ngoc Son (Jade Mountain) Temple (left), as a man folds his legs into the lotus position for meditation.

Since the 15th century, artisans' guilds have occupied the Old Quarter. Each was an independent body, with its own council of nobles. The streets were named for their particular trade: Rice Street, Paper Street and Silk Street, to name a few. Funerary objects, like these drums (above), have a street of their own, too.

Instruments of his own fashioning hang behind a musician as he plucks the strings of the dan tranh, or zither (left). One of the classical instruments of Vietnam, the 16-string zither is included in the collection of five instruments called "the five perfections".

Guild merchants await customers beside a neat collage of shrines and other votive objects (above).

A grandmother minds the baby and the antique shop (left). Ceramics, lacquerware, opium pipes, basketry and religious statues are some of the old goods on offer.

At Bat Trang, on the Red River outside Hanoi, a woman tests the dryness of round cakes of coal (above). Still a prime source of fuel, coal is at least partially responsible for the haze that frequently blankets the capital.

Though resembling nothing so much as a pile of rubble, the stones are in fact raw material for successful — if slow — road mending. The workers labour under the gaze of passengers in a typically fully laden bus (top right). Bricks are stacked in baskets hung from a bamboo pole and then carried to the kiln, in Ha Son province (right).

Dog is considered a delicacy in Vietnam, where there are restaurants specializing in the preparation of dog meat. The animals are bred and sold at markets like this one west of Hanoi (above).

Transporting goods to the market can be a laborious and time-consuming process. The ubiquitous bicycle (right) serves as a family car and pickup truck.

A class rehearses a traditional dance at Hanoi Dance School (top).
At once confident and anxious, a boy plays the dan nguyet for his examiner at the Hanoi School of
Music (above).

A young man practises a folk dance (left). Each movement is precise and
meaningful, adhering to timeless tradition.

Boys bring water buffalo in from the fields. Overhead, the sun does battle with ashen-hued clouds, throwing an eerie haze over the northern karst landscape.

The gentle, sculpted undulations of rice terraces fill the valleys and fields among the limestone spires of Vietnam's far north (above).

As they have done for four centuries, tradespeople of Bat Trang, on the Red River, ship the products of their ceramics cottage industry to market (following pages). The silty, alluvial soil washed through the north by the Red River not only waters the fields, it produces a clay well suited for pottery.

Legend says the bewitching karst landscape of Halong Bay, on the Gulf of Tonkin, came into being when a dragon living in the mountains ran pellmell towards the sea. His tail carved deep craters in the land which were filled with rushing water when he threw himself into the Gulf. The aptly named Cave of Marvels (left) is one of the myriad caves amid the 3,000 islands speckling the turquoise waters (above).

Reptiles clamber over each other, seeking their preferred sunning spot (above). Vietnam's animal kingdom is strikingly diverse, with 273 species of mammals, 773 species of birds, 180 species of reptiles and 80 species of amphibians.

Snake wine (left), and, during winter, snake soup, are believed to have medicinal qualities, not least of which is a supposed aphrodisiacal power. Snake oil is also commonly used in herbal remedies.

Hue

Straddling the banks of the Huong (Perfume) River, Hue is often called Vietnam's intellectual capital, and has earned descriptions of "cool" and "aloof" to match such a reputation.

CITY OF GREAT RULERS

L et's first dispose of a few figures. With 350,000 inhabitants, Hue is the smallest of the three historical capitals of Vietnam. Located only 12 kilometres from the sea, it covers 6,720 hectares. It is divided into 28 districts and 5 communes. There are 135 pagodas in the surrounding province, including three national pagodas. And in 1992, Hue was visited by 20,000 tourists.

Before Hue became the capital of a unified Vietnam in 1802, it already had a long and often tumultuous history. In the second century BC it was the headquarters of a Chinese garrison, and was known as Tay Quyen. A few centuries later, under the name K'iu Sou, it became the capital of a principality ruled by local warlords. Between the 10th and 14th centuries, the city was part of the Kingdom of Champa, maybe even at times its capital, and was attacked on many occasions by the northern kings. In 1306, through the marriage of Princess Huyen Tran, sister of King Tran Anh Tong,

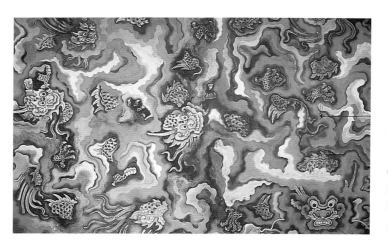

to King Che Man of Champa, the area finally became part of Vietnam and was later named Phu Xuan.

One of the three "Tay Son" brothers, Nguyen Hue, settled in Phu Xuan. After his death, Nguyen Anh, a sovereign of the Nguyen dynasty, took back the city with the assistance of the French and it became the imperial capital of Vietnam. Nguyen Anh adopted the symbolic title of Gia Long. A

Elaborate painted murals cover the ceiling of Khai Dinh's tomb.

Frenchman, Olivier de Puymanel, designed the famous Citadel and gave the city its present appellation.

King Trieu Tri (1841–1847) explained Hue's attributes as a capital by the fact that the city occupied a strategic position protected by mountains and rivers and was "better defended by nature than any other location, with the most solid gates in the world".

The construction of the Citadel, inspired by similar Vauban-styled military buildings designed in France, started in 1805 and lasted more than 20 years. According to contemporary chronicles, from 50,000 to 80,000 people toiled on the edifice each day. Inside the Citadel is the imperial city. Like the Citadel, it suffered greatly from the fighting that engulfed the centre of the former capital during the Tet Offensive of 1968. The National Liberation Front took over Hue and managed to keep its flag flying over the

King's Knight (Le Cavalier du Roi), the highest tower, for 25 days. Of relatively recent construction, the tower was destroyed when American forces regained control of the city after weeks of intensive bombing and door-to-door combat.

The imperial and the forbidden cities were partly reduced to rubble. In recent years, with the assistance of UNESCO, part of the historical Hue is being rebuilt or restored, and the development of tourism should encourage the authorities to restore Hue to its past royal grandeur.

Despite the devastation wreaked by the war, Hue remains the most poetic and most delightful city in Vietnam. The outskirts of the old capital, with the Perfume River and gentle hills, are one of the great natural beauties of the country. As the former director general of UNESCO, Mr Amadou Mahthar M'bow, said, "Hue is a masterpiece of urban poetry ... a city of perfect harmony."

Regarded as the least attractive of the Nguyen tombs, Khai Dinh's resting spot uncomfortably blends Eastern and European aspects.

If the King's Knight Tower no longer exists, the Tower of the Source of Happiness (Phuoc Duyen), built by Emperor Thieu Tri, still stands not far from the Pagoda of the Old Mistress of Heaven. Nearby temples, the Pavilion of the Great Hero, the temples of Quan Vo, the God of War, and of Quan Am, the Goddess of Compassion, reflect the dual religious heritage of Vietnam: Buddhism from India, and Confucianism along with Taoism from China.

Probably no other city or region in Vietnam has been more influenced by China than what used to be called Annam, of which Hue was the capital. In the 15th century, the victorious Chinese imposed on central Vietnam their culture and political organization. Chinese schools were established, and the study of Chinese classical literature was made compulsory. Much was done by the invaders to destroy local customs and culture. The pressure was such that it brought about a strong anti-Chinese reaction which benefited King Le Loi. However, Le Loi and other Vietnamese rulers and emperors were keen to maintain most of the political organization introduced by the Chinese conquerors.

Hue was the capital of the Nguyen, and the tombs of the Nguyen emperors along the Perfume River are among the most precious monuments of the city, an open textbook on the royal history of Vietnam and the way it was administered. The first tomb is that of Gia Long, the founder of the Nguyen dynasty, located about 16 kilometres upriver from the city.

Only the tomb of the last emperor who died in Vietnam, Khai Dinh, is not in the traditional imperial fashion, but rather a bizarre mixture of modern European and Vietnamese styles. The tomb of Minh Mang, who had no less than 142 children, is impressive, guarded by life-size statues of mandarins, lions and elephants. The monuments of Hue and the traditions of the Nguyen court have been the subject of intensive research. Much of it was published in the famous *Bulletin des Amis du Vieux Hue*, a learned journal started in 1914, which represents some of the best of France's contribution to an understanding of Vietnam's rich past.

The Nguyen kings have been much criticized because of their rigid conception of Confucianism, their social arrogance, and the fact they surrendered to the French colonial power. France and other European nations complained that the successor of Gia Long, King Minh Mang, was anti-Christian, rejecting Western influence. But as Huu Ngoc has remarked, history is never simple. Minh Mang and many of the Nguyens were effective administrators. And the last emperor, Bao Dai, who was crowned in 1926 at the age of 12, was never the puppet described by some of his earlier critics.

A display of the Royal Family's traditional dress, outside Thai Hoa Palace (left).

The women of Hue are said to be the most beautiful in all Vietnam (right).

In 1945, after the Communists took control of Hanoi and northern Vietnam, Bao Dai abdicated and handed over the imperial seal to Ho Chi Minh. He became a Supreme Counsellor of the new regime, under the name of Prince Vinh Thuy. He returned to power in 1948, but was deposed by Ngo Dinh Diem in 1954. He has lived in exile in France ever since.

For all its beauty and charm, its reputation as a wellspring of song and poetry, Hue has also been at the centre of Buddhist resistance against abuses of power from the central government. The car used by the monk who immolated himself in 1963 has been preserved near celebrated Thien Mu Pagoda (Temple of the Goddess of Compassion), and displayed with the photograph that hit the world's press, as a clear symbol that Hue's passions have encompassed the political and moral as well as the cultural.

The tranquil location of Tu Duc's tomb (left) is in direct contrast to how the ruler lived. When his elder brother revolted against his ascension to the throne, Tu Duc put his sibling and his family to death. Construction of his massive tomb complex, which he called Eternity, claimed the lives of many labourers, prompting these lines:
"What kind of eternity is this Eternity?
Its walls are built of soldiers' bones.
Its moats are filled with the blood of the people."

The gate to the tomb of Minh Mang, of the Nguyen dynasty, who ruled from 1820 to 1840 (top). East gate to the Citadel (above). Inside this small, walled city is the Imperial City and within that, the Forbidden City, where the emperor's family lived.

A young monk absorbs the serenity of the Thien Mu Pagoda sanctuary (above). The pagoda's origins are shrouded in myth: legend says a Fairy Woman (Thien Mu) appeared to Nguyen Lord Nguyen Hoang, governor of Thuan Hoa province, and ordered him to build a pagoda on this site. The buildings have been destroyed and restored many times since, but the eight-storey tower (right), built in 1844, has come to epitomize Hue's famed beauty.

Mandarin honour guards keep silent vigil at Khai Dinh's tome (left). Emperor from 1916 until his death in 1925, Khai Dinh attempted to modernize Vietnam and to gain autonomy from France. His reinforced concrete tomb is the least impressive of the Nguyen imperial tombs in Hue, and is held up as an example of the decline of Vietnamese culture during colonization. Buddhist monks near the Citadel (above), as dusk falls over the Perfume River, turning the darkening sky rose-purple.

Houseboats cluster together in a waterborne community on the Perfume River (following pages). Come daybreak, the river will be alive with the daily bustle of sampans and other craft.

Vietnam stretches some 1,600 kilometres north to south, the twisted coastline meandering for over 2,200 kilometres. In amongst the curves and bends are some of the region's most spectacular beaches, such as Dai Lanh, 80 kilometres north of Nha Trang (left). Delicate wisps of cloud hover over Lang Co (above). The gorgeous peninsula, with its seemingly endless beach and crystal-clear lagoon, completes the picture of an earthly paradise.

As the sky over Bai Truoc glows a rich gold, the sampan-studded sea is at peace. It is at this Vung Tau beach that local fisherpeople bring in their catch, spending the daylight hours cleaning and repairing their equipment.

The last moments of daylight are stained plum-purple and russet, as a farmer trundles his cart back to his home in Hoi An (above).

In the days when Hoi An was a thriving international port, many nationalities participated in the town's erstwhile success. Japanese, Chinese and Portuguese merchants, sailors and missionaries all took up residence. Each nationality left its architectural mark. The Japanese Bridge (following pages) was built between 1593 and 1596. A small pagoda in the centre was dedicated to "the monster that trembles the earth" — the earthquake.

Steam engines still run on Vietnam's metre-gauge rails; serviceable remnants of the colonial era (above). Travellers on the Hanoi-Saigon express while away the many hours of travel — the 1,798-kilometre journey can take between 30 and 50 hours (left). The word "express" is a bit of a misnomer: fast trains generally manage speeds of only about 30-40 kilometres per hour. The Hanoi-Saigon line itself took nearly four decades to complete — from 1899 to 1936.

An ancient bus picks up countryside-bound passengers in Danang (left). As crowded as the interior gets, the vehicle's roof will be equally loaded down — with bicycles, baskets of animals and food, goods for sale and goods newly purchased (above).

*Bountiful and beautiful seas provide Nha Trang (preceding pages) with dual economic punch:
fishing and tourism. A large fishing fleet, busy port, fish-breeding and oceanic research institutes all
promote the harvest of the sea. Tourists laze on the municipal beach, eat platefuls of delicious seafood
and indulge in snorkelling and scuba diving. A temporary carpet of fishing nets
carpets Hai Duang Beach (above).*

Against a backdrop of breaking waves, two boys, their heads bent in concentration, apply themselves to the task of repairing nets.

Packages of newspaper-wrapped tobacco resemble the smoking products they are destined to become (top). Tobacco plants are cosseted in a nursery (above), in Lam Dong province. When they reach a certain size, they will be transplanted to an open field.

At a silkworm farm near Dalat, many thousands of the worms are cocooned between woven bamboo frames. The white clumps will be dyed, spun and woven into the shimmering fabric, which was first brought to Vietnam by the Chinese.

Ho Chi Minh City

Motorcycles, taxis and cyclos all jockey for space at this roundabout on Quang Trung Road.

PROUD CITY OF PROMISE

If Hanoi is politics and history, Hue poetry and nostalgia, Saigon epitomizes business and the future. As a metropolis, the city is still young: a vibrant port, a trading centre, the great financial hope of a country which is finally moving towards prosperity. Where Hanoi is introspective, taking its time, Saigon is open to the world, aggressive and outgoing.

In the 14th century, it was called Prey Nokor (The Village in the Forest, translated by some as the Forest of the Kingdom), a minor Khmer settlement with its own administration and militia. There was a fort, a governor, people of various ethnic origins, a small port on the Saigon River. By the 17th century, the court of Hue was using the port of Prey Nokor so

frequently for its own commercial enterprises that the Cambodians authorized Hue to establish its own customs post in the town. A century later, Hue and the Nguyen kings were in full control of the city; they renamed it Saigon.

The Chinese population, who were scattered in settlements along the river, grew as rapidly as Saigon's prosperity. In 1778, the Chinese regrouped in a sister city, Cholon, which to this day remains a bustling centre of commerce and finance con-

The Municipal Theatre, built 1899, and in the background the Continental Hotel, erected 1885.

nected to Hong Kong, Bangkok and Taipei by the invisible but strong links that unite members of extended Chinese families.

The development of Saigon and the appeal of its perfect location near the sea was such that in 1789, Saigon briefly replaced Hue as the capital of the Nguyen dynasty. King Nguyen Anh redesigned the layout of the city according to the precepts of Chinese geomancy, giving to his rule in the new capital a stamp of divine approval. When Nguyen Anh left Saigon for Hue in 1802, taking the name Gia Long, Saigon became the centre of an autonomous vice-royalty. Its boundaries included what was left of the once glorious kingdom of Champa and Cochinchina.

The son of Gia Long, Minh Mang, was less respectful of Saigon's identity and sense of independence. In 1833, the city rebelled, and in angry response, Minh Mang razed many of the proudest symbols of Saigon, killing and dispersing much of the population. As a French historian wrote, "The whole city cried out for a new urban identity. The psychological climate prepared the way for colonial intervention by the French in 1859."

The city today reflects a variety of influences, from Asian energy and commerce to grand French-inspired urban planning and scattered leftovers of the American presence. Because of its auspicious location, and the relative stability it enjoyed during the 1950s and 1960s, not to mention the artificial economic boom of the Vietnam war, Saigon prospered quickly. It could, in a not so distant future, rival Bangkok and Singapore in the quest for economic and financial supremacy in Southeast Asia, one of the world's fastest developing regions.

Saigon, once known as the Pearl of the Orient, was the capital of the Republic of South Vietnam from 1954 until its fall in April 1975. The city was renamed Ho Chi Minh in 1976. Barely 10 metres above sea level and only 3 kilometres from the ocean, it is the largest city in Vietnam, with 4.5 million inhabitants, 12 urban and 6 rural precincts, 60 wards and 700 street blocks. Its fairly chaotic expansion, especially during the years of the Vietnam war, followed no special urban plan, blurring the clearer map imprinted by history. The main Citadel, built by Nguyen Anh in 1790 and destroyed by Minh Mang in 1836, was rebuilt on a smaller scale before being completely demolished by the French in 1859. The red brick Notre

Shanty dwellings line the Saigon River.

Dame Cathedral was erected on the site of the Citadel's arsenal in 1880. Next to the cathedral is the central post office, resembling similar French edifices and giving the whole square a look that hesitates between latterday southern France and a tropical metropolis.

The former Rue Catinat, baptised Tu Do (Freedom) in 1954 and changed to Dong Khoi Street (Popular Uprising) in 1975, was at the heart of the French and then the American Saigon. Some of the main hotels are clustered in the area. The Continental, where Graham Greene conceived his *Quiet American*, one of the best Western novels about Vietnam, has been renovated recently, with plenty of marble. In front of the Continental, Givral, the city's most famous bakery, continues to offer delicious cookies and tiny cups of strong French-style coffee.

Across the square, the more recent Caravelle (built in 1958) over-looks the Municipal Theatre, inspired by the architecture of the Grand Palais in Paris. The theatre served as the seat of the National Assembly during the days of the South Vietnamese Republic. The nearby Rex Hotel has a lovely terrace and the best view over City Hall, the seat of Ho Chi Minh's People's Committee, another example of lavish French colonial architecture. At the bottom of Dong Khoi, the Majestic Hotel and its new terrace, the consequence of a fire that destroyed the fifth-floor restaurant in 1990, presents a spectacular view over the Saigon River. The Majestic offers another rare luxury: a suite with a view and a piano. On the right, along the river, the Ho Chi Minh Museum is set in the lovely old customs house. From here, in 1911, Ho Chi Minh sailed to France aboard the *Latouche-Treville.*

In the late 1970s and early 1980s, Saigon and Cholon experienced difficult times. The dogmatism of many Communist cadres sent from the north, the isolation of the country, a series of ill-planned economic reforms

and the accelerated pace of reunification turned this vibrant community into a sleepy, depressed municipality. During these years, thousands of people, many from Saigon and Cholon, fled the country in overloaded boats. Even in Dong Khoi Street there was hardly a shop or a restaurant worth mentioning, as most had closed down for lack of business. At times, Cholon looked like a vast abandoned settlement inhabited only by ghosts of the past.

The reforms favoured by the 6th and 7th Congress of the Communist Party found fertile ground in Saigon. In a few short years, dramatic changes took place. Cholon is once again the centre of the most important deal-making in Vietnam, alive with new and old restaurants, its markets full of goods, much of it smuggled from neighbouring China, Hong Kong and Singapore.

Built on the site of the Citadel Arsenal, Notre Dame Cathedral surveys a considerably more peaceful scene (right).
A fragile load is manoeuvred through the streets (left).

Saigon is once again a vibrant, cosmopolitan city fitting the description given more than 40 years ago by the anonymous writer of a tourist guide to the south:

"The rain falling on the city, the young cigarette vendor, the boy selling newspapers, the sampan sliding in the canal under the protection of two big eyes painted on the bow, the burial that doesn't let the sadness of the separation disturb the happiness of the living, and muster in a long procession of pennant-bearers, noisy musicians, one or more hearses, cyclos, bicycle riders, taxis, private cars, food and refreshments which are consumed on the way thinking of the deceased..."

Along with the economic boom has come advertising. One of the most popular methods of getting one's message across is the billboard (left). The Majestic Hotel's awning receives a sprucing-up (above).

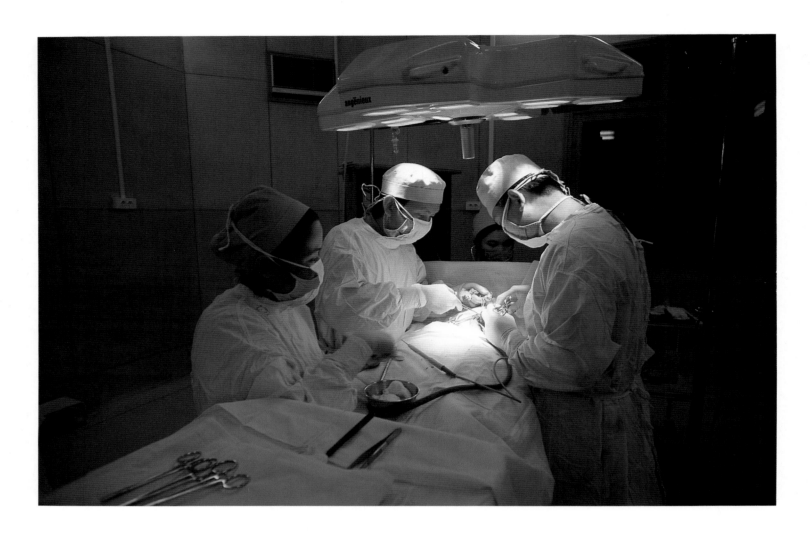

The health care network is controlled by the state and aims to provide treatment for anyone in need,
from public health centres in each village to specialized urban facilities. Grall Hospital,
staffed by French-speaking doctors and nurses, has enjoyed a reputation for quality
medical care for more than a century.

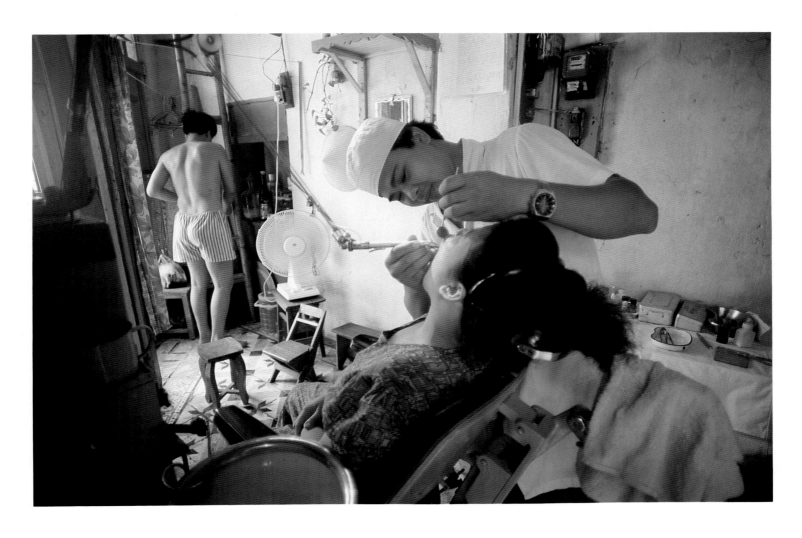

Despite a relatively modern health care system, many backstreet practitioners still attract a strong allegiance.

Barbells, dumbbells and weights surround two bodybuilders as they pump iron.
Gyms and fitness centres are proliferating in urban centres.

Wood shavings scatter at a carpenter's shop in Cholon (top left). About one-third of Vietnam's
manufacturing output is produced in Saigon and Cholon. The latter district was first settled by
Chinese merchants in the late 18th century and is still home to the country's biggest ethnic-Chinese
populace. A man repairs a moped on a Saigon sidewalk (left).

Nightlife in Ho Chi Minh City is as brash and fast-paced as its daytime persona. Sidewalk cafés (left) attract folk who like to talk; flashing lights and a pounding beat suit those who prefer to dance (above and left).

France earned few kudos for the way in which it assumed its role as colonizer, yet its architectural legacy is undoubtedly one of the country's most charming aspects. From provincial-style villas to grand edifices, few can resist their charm.

Mediterranean colours enliven some colonial buildings (top right); the Neo-Romanesque Notre Dame Cathedral (top left) was built in 1880, but the spires were added in 1900. Graceful balconies are popular vantage points for the never-ending fascination with people watching (left).

Brightly painted shopfront awnings in Cholon may provide shelter from the sun, but not always from advertising (above).

A shaft of light pierces the murky darkness of the Emperor of Jade Pagoda (above). Also known as the Tortoise Pagoda, it was used as a meeting place for Chinese secret societies plotting to overthrow the Manchu dynasty who held power in Peking.

Spirals of joss, hanging from the ceiling of a temple in Ho Chi Minh City, cast heavy shadows (right).

Muslims pray at Central Saigon Mosque (following pages). Muslims make up about 0.5 percent of the population; their origins are thought to lie with Arab traders who journeyed to China, and likely Vietnam, in the 7th century. Although the Chams were converted to Islam, and indeed, still declare themselves to be Muslim, their religious practices are quite different and are more like thin dilutions of Muslim tradition.

The persistent image of Vietnam as a thoroughly wartorn nation is inaccurate, but not entirely so. The war may be over, but as a result of those years, many people fight daily their own personal battles (above).

Vendors at Vung Tao are well stocked, in anticipation of the weekend crowds (top left). On Sundays, especially, throngs of Vietnamese from Ho Chi Minh City descend on the peninsula for some well-deserved rest and recreation.

Comfortably ensconced on one of her rental items, a rubber ring vendor enjoys a nap (left).

Jockeys aged between 12 and 15 race for cheering crowds three days a week at Phu Tho race track (preceding pages). Daily turnover ranges in the neighbourhood of US$3,500.

Can Tho is the commercial and cultural nerve centre of the Mekong Delta (above). Situated in the heart of Vietnam's largest rice-producing area, the town exudes a profitable yet laidback air.

A gaggle of geese for sale at a poultry market in the Delta (right).

Rice is of supreme importance to the Vietnamese (top). New Year's rice cakes wrapped in banana leaves are reminders of the days when such bundles were carried by soldiers. No matter what the weather, the rice did not spoil and, eaten with whatever greens were available, it provided a balanced diet. A variety of fruit is grown in the region, including tangy grapes and succulent lychees (above).

Fish — whole, in pieces, and dried — is the other staple of the Mekong Delta (left).

Palm trees sway and puffy clouds drift across the sky on a breezy day,
Phu Quoc Island (above).

An old man and the sea; Phu Quoc Island (top left). A fishing trawler is
the centre of attention (left). Neighbouring Thailand is the island's main trading partner.

Chronology

208 BC - A former Chinese general takes over Au Lac, in North Vietnam, and proclaims himself emperor of Nam Viet.

1st century BC - Nam Viet is incorporated into the Chinese empire under the name Giao Chi.

AD 39 - Anti-Chinese revolt led by the Trung sisters.

939–967 - The Ngo dynasty.

967 - End of Chinese rule. Emperor Dinh Tien Hoang names the new independent state Dai Co Viet.

968–980 - The Dinh dynasty.

980–1009 - The Early Le dynasty.

1010–1225 - The Ly dynasty.

1010 - Foundation of Thang Long (Hanoi).

1225–1400 - The Tran dynasty.

1400–1428 - The Ho dynasty.

1428 - China recognizes the independence of Vietnam. Emperor Le Loi defeated the Chinese forces in 1427 after ten years of fighting.

1428–1776 - The Later Le dynasty.

1460–1498 - Reign of Emperor Le Thanh Tong. Period of important legal reforms. Territorial expansion towards the south.

1627 - Introduction of the new romanized system of writing by Bishop Alexandre de Rhodes and other foreign missionaries.

1772 - Start of the Tay Son rebellion.

1792–1883 - The Nguyen dynasty.

1802 - Nguyen Anh who had regained control over the country, thanks partly to foreign assistance, becomes emperor of Vietnam under the name Gia Long. The capital of unified Vietnam is moved to Hue.

1847 - French troops clash with Vietnam in Da Nang (then called Tourane). Tu Duc, the new emperor, rejects foreign influence and Christianity.

1861 - Capture of Saigon by the French.

1862 - Tu Duc is forced to sign a treaty with France granting her vast economic and political concessions.

1883 - Annam and Tonkin become French protectorates, Cochinchina a colony.

1887 - Creation of the Indochinese Union.

1890 - Birth of Ho Chi Minh in Central Vietnam.

1911 - Ho Chi Minh leaves Vietnam for France.

1925 - Bao Dai becomes emperor and then goes to France to finish his studies.

1922 - Ho Chi Minh leaves Paris for Moscow. The previous year, he had joined the French Communist Party.

1924 - Ho Chi Minh is sent to China (Canton) as an assistant to the famous Comintern agent Mikhail Borodin.

1932 - Bao Dai returns from France.

1941 - Ho Chi Minh returns to Vietnam for the first time since 1911. Foundation of the Viet Minh.

1944 - Foundation of the People's Army of Vietnam by Vo Nguyen Giap.

1945 - On 9 March, Japan takes over French administration in all of Indochina. Two days later, Bao Dai proclaims Vietnam's independence. Japan, defeated on 15 August, transfers power to the Viet Minh. Ho Cho Minh announces the creation of a provisional government on 18 August in Hanoi. Bao Dai abdicates on 23 August and becomes Supreme Counselor of the new regime.

1946 - France recognizes Vietnam as a free state within the French Union. But Admiral Thierry d'Argenlieu, France's High Commissioner for Indochina, creates a separate government in Cochinchina. In December, Viet Minh troops leave Hanoi. Beginning of the war.

1949 - Bao Dai signs an agreement with France: Vietnam is an associate state within the French Union.

1950 - Ho Chi Minh's Democratic Republic of Vietnam is recognized by China and the Soviet Union.

1951 - Foundation of the Lao Dong (Workers Party), successor of the Communist Party, which was officially dissolved in 1945.

1954 - French troops are defeated in Dien Bien Phu on 7 May. Geneva agreement in July. Bao Dai denounces the agreement. Vietnam is divided at the 17th parallel.

1964 - Gulf of Tonkin incident: an American destroyer, the *Maddox*, is attacked by a Vietnamese patrol boat. This becomes a pretext for increased American involvement in Vietnam.

1965 - On 8 March, two American marine battalions land in Danang. By the end of the year, 200,000 American troops are in Vietnam.

1968 - Tet Offensive begins on 31 January. In August, Lyndon Johnson announces an end to American bombing of Vietnam.

1969 - On 3 September, Ho Chi Minh dies in Hanoi.

1973 - A ceasefire agreement is signed in Paris between the United States and North Vietnam. The last American troops leave Vietnam in March.

1974 - The war continues between North and South Vietnam.

1975 - "Great Spring offensive" or "Ho Chi Minh campaign". Saigon is captured by Communist forces on 30 April, bringing an end to the war.

1976 - Reunification of Vietnam.

1979 - In February–March, Chinese troops invade Vietnam's northern provinces in retaliation for a Vietnamese military expedition to Cambodia.

1986 - In December, the 6th Congress of the Communist Party of Vietnam orders vast economic reforms.

Sponsors' Profiles

PEPSI-COLA INTERNATIONAL

"Pepsico is first and foremost a growth company. Today, our three divisions — Soft Drinks, Snack Foods and Restaurants — have 338,000 employees and US$20 billion of annual sales turnover. Our products are available in 150 countries. With the opening of our soft drinks operation in Vietnam, we are introducing Pepsi-Cola products to a new generation of consumers. Here in Southeast Asia, market conditions are ripe for expansion, with the rising standard of living and opening of trade. Our goal is to take advantage of this emerging opportunity by investing now for future growth. This quest for rapid growth keeps us innovative, shaking things up, breaking down barriers — all in search of new opportunities.

We are proud to be at the forefront of economic development in Vietnam!"

OMNI SAIGON HOTEL VIETNAM

OMNI SAIGON HOTEL

Omni Saigon Hotel is the first deluxe international hotel to open in Ho Chi Minh City, providing a range of international facilities and services hitherto unavailable in Vietnam. The Hotel is also the first of a series of new developments in Asia for Omni Hotels Asia-Pacific which plans to bring its total number of hotels in this region to 20 by 1997. Omni Hotels have created a loyal following by offering high quality, people-oriented hotels to service businessmen and discriminating leisure travellers. Other hotels are planned for key business locations in the Asia-Pacific region complementing the group's hotels in Hong Kong, Singapore, Indonesia, China and, now, Vietnam.

Elsworth Books Ltd

Elsworth Books would like to thank the sponsors who have made this book possible. Elsworth Books is a dynamic publishing house currently focusing on illustrated books about Southeast Asia. Among our titles are *Cambodia — A Portrait* and *Return to the Heart of the Dragon*. Forthcoming titles include *Burma — A Portrait* and *The Philippines — A Portrait*. These books are all made possible by corporate sponsorship. Companies who would like to gain exposure through advertising in reprints and future titles are invited to contact our Hong Kong office:
Paul Andrews or Tim Hall
407 Yu Yuet Lai Building
43–55 Wyndham Street
Central
Hong Kong
Tel: (852) 530 2113
Fax: (852) 869 8467

Credits

Tim Hall:
Back cover
3, 4, 5, 6, 7, 10, 11, 28, 30, 31, 32, 34, 35 (top), 36, 37, 42, 43, 44, 45, 48, 50, 51, 52, 54, 55, 58 (top left), 60, 62 (top), 63 (bottom), 70, 71, 72, 76, 88, 90, 91, 94, 95, 101, 103, 104, 105, 106, 108, 109, 110, 111, 112 (top), 114, 115, 116, 117, 118, 119, 120, 121, 122, 123, 125, 126, 127, 128, 129, 136, 137, 140, 141, 142, 143, 144, 145, 146, 150, 151, 157, 159, 166, 167, 170, 171, 172, 176, 177, 178, 179, 180 (top), 181, 182, 183, 186, 187, 188, 189, 190, 191, 194, 194, 195, 196, 197

Alain Evrard:
29, 33, 39, 40, 41, 46, 47, 49, 53, 56, 57, 58 (top right, bottom right), 61, 62 (bottom), 63 (top), 68, 69, 77, 78, 80, 81, 82, 83, 84, 85, 89, 92, 93, 96, 112 (bottom), 113, 134, 135, 148, 149, 152, 154, 155, 156, 158, 162, 163, 164, 165, 168, 169, 173, 174, 175, 184, 193

Peter Charlesworth: Front cover
Sophie Neilan: Map illustration, 12
Tapabor: 14, 15, 16, 17, 18, 19, 20, 21, 22, 23, 24, 25
Gerhard Jören: 8, 9, 58 (bottom left), 73, 74, 75, 97, 100, 124, 132, 153, 180 (bottom), 185
Andy Soloman: 66, 107
Sarah Lock: 26, 27, 67, 160, 192
Apa: 35 (bottom), 38, 59, 64, 86, 87, 98, 99, 102
Manh Sinh: 130, 131
Flavie Staib: 65

Sponsors' Profiles

Vietnam Investment Review

VIETNAM INVESTMENT REVIEW

Vietnam Investment Review is the only foreign-managed English-language weekly business newspaper produced in Vietnam and circulated world-wide. From its offices in Hanoi and Ho Chi Minh City, a dedicated team of Vietnamese and foreign journalists consistently produce the most accurate and up-to-date information on this booming economy.

Serving authentic Vietnamese cuisine in a colonial French setting. A taste of VIetnam now as it was then.
2 California Tower, Lan Kwai Fong, Central, Hong Kong. Tel: 869 7399

DIETHELM TRAVEL

Diethelm Travel is one of the pioneers in developing tours throughout Indochina, with its own offices in Thailand, Laos, Cambodia and Vietnam. Diethelm Travel organizes tailor-made individual trips as well as escorted group tours with regular departures at competitive rates. For more information, please contact:

Diethelm Travel
Kian Gwan Building II
140/1 Wireless Road
Bangkok 10330
Thailand

Tel: (66 2) 255 9150-70
Fax: (66 2) 256 0248-9

TIGER BEER

Constantly rated as a premium-quality beer by connoisseurs around the world, Tiger Beer has been praised by the London *Sunday Times* for its "balance, clean taste and aroma". The *Washington Magazine*, meanwhile, voted it as "positively the best beer in the world".
Tiger Beer, to date, has won 25 international gold medals at the prestigious Monde Selection competitions. One of the world's most celebrated international beers, Tiger Beer is now brewed by Vietnam Brewery Limited in Ho Chi Minh City.

Bibliography

Azambré, Georges, "Hanoi, notes de Geographie Urbaine", in *Bulletin de la Société des Etudes Indochinoises*, Vol. XXX, No. 4 (1955), Saigon
Azambré, Georges, "Les Origines de Hanoi", in *Bulletin de la Société des Etudes Indochinoises*, Vol. XXXIII, No. 3 (1958), Saigon
Bouchot, Jean, *Documents pour servir à l'Histoire de Saigon* (1859–1865) Editions Albert Portail. Saigon, 1927
Buttinger, Joseph, *The Smaller Dragon, a Political History of Vietnam*, New York, Frederick A. Praeger, 1958
Cima, Ronald J. (ed.), *Vietnam, a Country Study*, Washington, D.C., Federal Research Division, Library of Congress, 1989
Durand, Maurice and Pierre Huard, *Connaissance du Vietnam*, Ecole Française d'Extrême Orient, Hanoi, 1954
Etudes Vietnamiennes: Hanoi, des origines au 19e siecle, No. 48 (1977), Hanoi
Etudes Vietnamiennes: Hue, passé et present (1), No. 37 (1973)
Etudes Vietnamiennes: Hue, passé et present (2), No. 83 (1986) (new series), Hanoi

Farrère, Claude, *Mes Voyages, La Promenade d'Extrême Orient*, Paris, Ernest Flammarion, 1924
Huu Ngoc, "The Vietnamese Soul in Popular Literature", in *Vietnamese Studies*, No. 71 (new series, No. 1) (1983) Hanoi
Huu Ngoc and Françoise Correze, *Anthologie de la Literature Vietnamienne*, Paris, L'Harmattan, 1982
Huu Ngoc and Françoise Correze, *Anthology of Vietnamese Popular Literature*, Hanoi, Foreign Languages Publishing House, 1984
Huu Ngoc and Nguyen Khac Vien, *Vietnamese Literature*, Hanoi, Foreign Languages Publishing House, no date given
Huu Ngoc and Nguyen Khac Vien, *Anthologie de la Literature Vietnamienne*, Hanoi, Editions en Langues Etrangères
Karnov, Stanley, *Vietnam, A history*, New York, The Viking Press, 1983
Masson, André, *Histoire du Vietnam. Coll. Que Sais-je?* Paris, Presse Universitaire de France, 1949
Nepote, Jacques and Xavier Guillaume, *A Guide to Vietnam*, Bangkok, Asia Books Co., 1992

Nguyen Du Kieu, Traduction de Nguyen Khac Vien, presentation de Nguyen Tien Chung, Hanoi, Editions en Langues Etrangères, 1974
Nguyen Khac Vien, *Vietnam, une Longue Histoire*, Hanoi, Editions en Langues Etrangères, 1987
Nguyen Van Huyen, *La Civilisation Annamite*, Collection de la direction de l'instruction publique de l'Indochina, Saigon, 1944
Tran Van Da and Nguyen Phuc Khanh (eds.), *Vietnam, My Homeland*, Hanoi, Su That and Vietnam Tourism, 1989
Vietnamese Studies: Van Mieu-Quoc Tu Giam, The Temple of Literature, special issue, March 1991, Hanoi
Vietnamese Studies: The Traditional Village, No. 61 (1979), Hanoi
Vietnamese Studies: Confucian Scholars in Vietnamese History, No. 56 (1979), Hanoi
West, Helen (ed.), *Vietnam. Insight Guides*, Hong Kong, APA Publications, 1993
XXX Guide Touristique, Laos, Cambodge, Vietnam, Saigon, Editions C.L., 1957 (the book covers only South Vietnam and includes an English and a Vietnamese translation of the original French)